Zone Diet Cookbook

Includes 50 Zone Diet Recipes For Every Meal

Table Of Contents:

Introduction

Welcome to the Zone, a new healthy diet that will positively impact your health physically, mentally, and spiritually. These recipes are not only healthy meal alternatives but also taste delicious. All 50 recipes have been selected to deliver top-notch results and allow you to have a wide variety of tasty meal options.

You will see recipes for every meal – breakfast, lunch, snacks, dinner, and even desserts. You can mix and match them as you please. Who says dieting means starving? Tired of eating the same meal over and over? This cookbook allows you to have a wide variety of meals that will always please your taste buds.

Chapter 1 HEARTY BREAKFAST

Lime Raspberry Smoothie

Ingredients

- 1 cup raspberries
- 1 cup one percent milk
- ½ cup yogurt, 0% fat
- Juice of one lime
- 3 tablespoons slivered almonds

Preparation

- Mix all ingredients in a blender until smooth.

Blueberry Cottage Cheese

Ingredients

- 1 teaspoon extra virgin olive oil
- ¾ cup cottage cheese, low fat
- ½ cup frozen or fresh blueberries
- ½ cup applesauce, unsweetened
- 5 teaspoons slivered almonds

Preparation

- Mix the applesauce, olive oil, and cheese in a small bowl, then add the almond and blueberries.

Apple Jumble Zinger

Ingredients

- One apple

- Six egg whites, hard boiled the previous night

- 1 ½ tablespoons of raw ginger

- 1 cup strawberries

- 1 teaspoon extra virgin olive oil

Preparation

- The night before, hard-boil the eggs then discard the yolks.

- Mix all the ingredients in a blender until they're like chunky cereal in size.

Breakfast Mousse

Ingredients

- 1 cup diced strawberries
- 1 cup zero-fat yogurt
- 2/3 cup blueberries
- 5 macadamia nuts

Preparation

- Mix all ingredients in a blender until smooth.

Crunchy Delight

Ingredients

- ½ chopped apple
- ¾ cup cottage cheese, low fat
- ½ cup sliced strawberries
- ½ cup sliced celery
- 3 tablespoons chopped almonds
- ½ cup blueberries

Preparation

- Put the cottage cheese in a large bowl.

- Add the cut fruits and sprinkle with almonds.

Fruity Nutty

Ingredients

- ¾ cup cottage cheese, low fat

- ½ piece pear

- ¾ cup sliced celery

- 1/2 cup sliced strawberries

- ½ piece chopped and peeled kiwi

- 1/8 cup chopped walnuts

Preparation

- In a large bowl, add the cottage cheese. Add the cut fruits afterwards.

- Sprinkle with walnuts

Frozen Blueberry Yogurt

Ingredients

- 4 ice cubes
- ¾ cup plain yogurt, low fat
- ½ cup cottage cheese, low fat
- ¾ cup frozen blueberries
- 1 tsp. vanilla
- 2 tablespoons slivered almonds
- ¼ artificial sweetener

Preparation

- Mix all ingredients in a blender until smooth.

Speedy Breakfast

Ingredients

- One large apple, cut into bite-size pieces
- 3 ½ teaspoons peanut butter
- ¾ cup cottage cheese, low fat

Preparation

- In a medium-sized bowl, add the cottage cheese, followed by the peanut butter and apple.

Oats and Yogurt

Ingredients

- 1 teaspoon agave nectar
- 1/3 cup cooked oats, steel cut
- 1 cup zero-fat yogurt
- 3 tablespoons chopped almonds
- 1/3 cup blueberries

Preparation

- Add all the ingredients together in a medium sized bowl then mix.

Berry Mix

Ingredients

- 4 teaspoons tahini
- 1 ½ cups mixed berries
- 2 ice cubes
- 3 scoops zone protein powder

Preparation

- Mix all ingredients in a blender until smooth.

Orange Apple Shake

Ingredients

- ½ cup each of apple and orange sections
- 1 cup 2% milk
- 14 grams protein powder

Preparation

- Put all the ingredients in the blender until they're fully blended.

Italian omelet

Ingredients

- 1 teaspoon olive oil
- 4 egg whites
- 1 oz. prosciutto
- 1 tablespoon low-fat cheese
- Salt and pepper

Directions

- Scramble the eggs in olive oil then add cheese and prosciutto. Add salt and pepper.

Chapter 2 SUMPTUOUS LUNCH

Chicken Fingers

Ingredients

- 1 tablespoon sesame seeds

- 1 ½ ounces chicken breast, skinned and deboned

- 2 tablespoons egg whites

Directions

- Preheat the oven to 350°F.

- Rinse the chicken, pat dry, and cut into strips, then dip in the egg whites and roll in sesame seeds.

- Place the coated strips on a nonstick baking sheet (sprayed with cooking oil).

- Bake for eighteen to twenty minutes until cooked.

Seafood and Chicken Salad Delight

Ingredients

- One oz. cooked shrimp
- One oz. cooked bay scallops
- One oz. canned salmon, flaked
- ½ cup scallion, thinly sliced
- 1 ½ tablespoons light mayonnaise
- ¼ teaspoon dried dill
- One teaspoon hot pepper sauce
- ¼ cup grated radishes
- ½ cup grated cucumber
- 1/8 teaspoon cayenne pepper
- 2 tablespoons chopped fresh cilantro
- 3 cups shredded lettuce
- ½ cup diced tomato
- ¾ cup green and red pepper strips
- ¼ cup snow peas

Directions

- Blend the scallops, scallions, shrimp, salmon, dill, hot pepper sauce, and light mayonnaise in a medium sized bowl.

- In another bowl, mix the cilantro, cucumber, cayenne, and radishes, then combine with lettuce, peppers, tomatoes, and snow peas. Top with the seafood mixture.

Turkey Salad

Ingredients

- ½ apple

- ½ cucumber, chopped

- 12 olives, chopped

- 2 ounces turkey breast – cooked and chopped

- ½ cup celery

- 2 tablespoon herb dressing

- 1/3 cup chopped red onion

Preparation

- In a large bowl, combine the apple and veggies.

- Toss with dressing then add the turkey.

Stir Fry Spicy Tofu

Ingredients

- 1 ½ teaspoons olive oil – divided

- 6 ounces extra firm tofu

- 1/8 teaspoon celery salt

- 1/3 cup thinly sliced onion

- ¾ cup bean sprouts

- ½ cup chopped celery

- ½ cup diced red bell pepper

- ½ cup sliced radishes

- 1 cup water – divide into two

- 1 tablespoon soy sauce

- ¼ teaspoon chili powder

- 1 tablespoon cider vinegar

- 2 tablespoons freshly squeezed lemon juice

Directions

- Heat oil in a medium sized sauté pan, stir in the celery salt, and add the tofu. Stir-fry until brown and crusted.

- Cook the veggies in another pan until tender, and then add water. Cover to steam.

- In a saucepan, add soy sauce, ½ cup water, and spices, heating to a light boil. Stir constantly then add the tofu.

- Add the sauce and tofu to the vegetables. Simmer for two to three minutes.

Applesauce Burgers with Spinach Salad

Ingredients

- 1/3 cup unsweetened applesauce
- 2 teaspoons dehydrated onion flakes
- Dressing and Spinach salad
- 3 oz. ground chicken breast
- 2 teaspoons vinegar
- 1 ½ teaspoons olive oil
- 1 teaspoon fruit preserve
- 2 teaspoons water
- Salt and pepper
- 2 slices roughly chopped onion
- 3 cups baby spinach – tear the stems off
- ½ tomato – cut into pieces
- ½ cup strawberries – chunked

Directions

- Preheat the broiler then mix the onions, egg whites, and applesauce in a bowl.

- Add the turkey, mix well, and shape into a burger.

- Place the burger on the rack then broil for 5 minutes. Flip the burgers then broil for another five minutes, or until the meat is cooked.

- Heat the remaining applesauce. Serve it over the burgers.

- Whisk the dressing ingredients with the mashed strawberries. Afterwards, mix onion, spinach, strawberries, and tomato in a bowl.

Chicken Barbecue Salad

Ingredients

- 3 oz. deboned and diced chicken breast
- 2 teaspoons olive oil
- ¼ cup diced onions
- 1 ½ cup stripped bell peppers
- 1/8 teaspoon cider vinegar
- 2 cups shredded cabbage
- 1 teaspoon minced garlic
- 3 cups lettuce
- ½ cup barbecue sauce
- Salt and pepper

Directions

- Add oil, pepper, chicken breast, onion, vinegar, and garlic in a sauté pan, and then add barbecue sauce. Continue until cooked.

- Simmer and cover for 5 minutes, until the mixture is hot. Next, blend the cabbage and lettuce then place on a plate.

- Spoon the vegetable mixture and the chicken over the salad mixture. Lastly, add pepper and salt.

Chicken Teppanyaki

Ingredients

- 1 sweet bell pepper
- 3 oz. boneless chicken breast
- ½ cup chopped onion
- ½ cup frozen or fresh green beans
- 2 ½ teaspoon of olive oil
- 1 cup sliced mushroom
- ¾ cup tomato sauce
- 1 tablespoon soy sauce
- 1 cup cooked spaghetti squash

Directions

- Cut the chicken into small squares then slice the veggies.
- Heat oil in the pan in medium heat then cook the chicken.
- Add the soy sauce, veggies, and tomato sauce then cook for ten minutes.
- Scoop it over the cooked spaghetti squash.

Chunky Ham Salad

Ingredients

- 2 teaspoons rice vinegar
- 1 ½ tablespoons freshly-squeezed lemon juice
- 1 teaspoon water
- 2/3 teaspoon extra virgin olive oil
- 3 cups torn lettuce
- Salt and pepper
- ½ cucumber, sliced
- ¼ cup sliced onion
- 6 cherry tomatoes, halved
- 5 oz. turkey ham
- ¼ grapes, halved

Directions

- In a small jar, mix the first five dressing ingredients a few hours in advance, shaking it often.
- Mix the remaining ingredients together to make the salad.

Curried Spinach with Tofu

Ingredients

- 10 cups fresh spinach
- ½ teaspoon cumin
- 1 tablespoon olive oil
- 2 tablespoons minced hot chilies
- 2 tablespoons soy sauce
- 10 oz. of light firm tofu
- 1 tablespoon minced ginger
- Salt and pepper
- ¼ cup chopped fresh cilantro
- 1 teaspoon curry powder
- 1/4 teaspoon nutmeg
- ½ teaspoon cinnamon

Directions

- Heat some oil in a skillet. Add the soy sauce, cumin, chilies, tofu, and ginger. Add salt and pepper.
- Sauté over high heat then add the cilantro, spinach, cream cheese, and curry powder.

Grilled Sausage Salad

Ingredients

- 1/2 teaspoon olive oil
- Cooking spray
- 2 tablespoons freshly squeezed lemon juice
- 2 tablespoons unsalted vegetable stock
- 1 red bell pepper cut in half
- Salt and pepper
- 1 cup zucchini, cut lengthwise
- ¾ cup red onion, cut in half
- 1 ½ pcs. sweet Italian sausage, ½-inch-thick slices
- 1 cup summer squash, cut lengthwise

Directions

- Preheat the grill.
- Spray the cut veggies with olive oil spray, and then combine salt and pepper, vegetable stock, and lemon juice in a bowl. Add the veggies.
- Stir to coat. Use cooking spray on a grill topper.

- Spray cooking oil on the veggies and add the sliced sausage to the heated grill topper.

Pork Marinara

Ingredients

- 3 ½ oz. Pork tenderloin, sliced thinly
- 1 ½ olive oil
- Salt and pepper
- ½ cup diced onion
- 1 clove minced garlic
- 2 cups asparagus, steamed and sliced
- 1 can dice tomato with juice (14.5 oz.)
- 2 cups cauliflower, steamed (mashed)

Directions

- Heat oil in the skillet, and then add the onion, pork, salt, and pepper.
- Cook until both sides of the pork are lightly browned then add tomatoes and garlic. Cook for ten minutes then add the cauliflower and asparagus.
- Cook for another five to eight minutes.

Steak and Veggie Medley

Ingredients

- 10 oz. frozen spinach
- 2 tablespoons unsalted vegetable stock
- 1 cup chopped tomatoes
- ¼ cup frozen pearl onions
- 1 clove minced garlic
- ¼ cup kidney beans, drained and rinsed
- 1/8 teaspoon celery salt
- 2 teaspoon cider vinegar
- Salt and pepper
- ½ teaspoon chopped parsley
- 3 oz. sirloin steak, ¾ inch thick
- ½ kiwi, sliced
- ½ teaspoon olive oil

Directions

- In a medium pan, heat the spinach, tomatoes, stock, onions, seasonings, and beans. Sauté for five to seven minutes or until everything's crispy.

- In another pan, sauté the steak until it is cooked to the desired degree.

- Garnish with slices of kiwi.

Chapter 3 WONDERFUL SNACK ATTACK

Fruit Delight

Ingredients

- 1 apple, chopped

- 1 ½ cups chopped celery

- 1 cup sliced strawberry

- 1 cup cottage cheese, low fat

Preparation

- Mix the cut ingredients in a small bowl then add cheese.

Cacao Strawberry Yogurt

Ingredients

- 1 12/ tablespoon cacao powder
- ¼ cup fat free yogurt
- ¼ cup sliced strawberry

Preparation

- Stir the cacao powder into the yogurt, and then gently stir in the strawberry.

Fruity Cheese

Ingredients

- 1 plum
- 1 low fat cheese stick
- Preparation
- Mix the plum and cheese stick together.

Yogurt Cucumber

Ingredients

- 1 cup chunked cucumber
- ¼ cup fat free yogurt
- 2 tablespoons freshly-squeezed lemon juice

Preparation

- Mix the cucumber with the yogurt then add lemon juice.

Cold milk

Ingredients

- 4 tablespoon low-fat powdered milk
- Artificial sweetener
- Water

Preparation

- Add the powdered milk and sweetener into the water.

Horseradish Slaw

Ingredients

- ½ teaspoon pepper
- 2 tablespoons fat free yogurt
- ½ cup shredded cabbage
- ½ tablespoon horseradish

Preparation

- Combine yogurt, horseradish, and pepper in a bowl then add cabbage.

Shrimp and Sauce

Ingredients

- 2 ½ tablespoons cocktail sauce

- 1 ½ oz. frozen previously cooked shrimp

- 1 ½ horseradish

- ½ teaspoon extra virgin olive oil

Directions

- Submerge the shrimp in cold water for ten minutes.

- Add the cocktail sauce, olive oil, and horseradish in a small bowl. Start dipping once the shrimp has thawed.

Chapter 4 DELECTABLE DINNER

Almond Chicken

Ingredients

- 2 cups steamed broccoli flowerets
- 3 oz. sliced boneless chicken breast
- 1 green bell pepper, chopped
- 1 red bell pepper, chopped
- ¾ cup chopped onion
- 1 cup cherry tomatoes, halved
- 1 clove garlic, minced
- 2 teaspoon sliced almonds
- Salt and pepper

Directions

- Steam the broccoli.
- Heat olive oil in a sauté pan. Add the green and red bell peppers, garlic, chicken, and onion.
- Sauté until both the chicken and veggies are cooked. Add the steamed broccoli and tomatoes. Top with almonds.

Baked Tilapia with Veggies

Ingredients

- 3 oz. Tilapia
- Cooking spray
- 1 ½ cups medium sized zucchini, sliced
- ¾ cup sliced tomato
- ¾ cup sliced bell pepper
- Salt and pepper
- ¾ cup sliced red onion
- 1 ½ teaspoons extra virgin olive oil

Directions

- Preheat oven to 350°F.
- Place the fish and sliced veggies in the bake ware sprayed with cooking oil spray. Sprinkle on salt and pepper.
- Bake for twenty to twenty five minutes or until the fish flakes, and then drizzle with oil.

Stir Fry Beef and Barley

Ingredients

- 1/8 cup pearled barley
- 1 teaspoon olive oil
- ½ tomato, sliced
- ½ cup chopped onion
- 3.5 oz. lean ground beef
- 1 cup frozen green beans
- ½ cup mushrooms
- ½ teaspoon soy sauce, low sodium
- 1/8 cup unsalted vegetable stock

Directions

- Cook the barley. Slice tomato then set aside.
- Heat oil in a large skillet. Add the beef. Stir until browned.
- Add green beans, mushrooms, and onions. Cook until the beans are crisp and tender.
- Stir in soy sauce and vegetable stock with the cooked barley. Add to the veggies and meat.

Chickpeas with Shrimp

Ingredients

- 1 tablespoon chipotle chili in adobo sauce

- 1 tablespoon olive oil

- 1 cup minced red onion

- 1 jalapeno pepper, minced and seeded

- 1 ½ cups chopped tomatoes

- ½ clove minced garlic

- 1 ½ freshly-squeezed lime juice

- ¼ cup canned garbanzo beans, drained

- 1/8 cup fresh cilantro, chopped

- Salt and pepper

- 3.5 oz. previously cooked and thawed shrimp

Directions

- Whisk together chipotle, garlic, olive oil, red onion, and jalapeno in a big bowl.

- Mix lime juice, garbanzo beans, tomato, and cilantro.

- Refrigerate for two hours. Serve with shrimp.

Turkey Tips Barbecue with Spinach

Ingredients

- 2 ½ cooked turkey breast
- 2 teaspoon olive oil
- ½ cup salsa
- 1/3 cup barbecue sauce
- 3 cups fresh spinach
- ½ garbanzo beans, rinsed
- ½ cup chopped onion

Directions

- Heat oil then add turkey and blend in salsa, barbecue sauce, and onion.
- Simmer for three to five minutes. Arrange spinach on a serving plate. Sprinkle with the garbanzo beans then top with turkey mixture.

Old-Fashioned Cabbage Soup

Ingredients

- 2/3 cup finely diced celery
- 1 chipotle chorizo chicken sausage, sliced
- ½ cup finely diced onions
- 1/8 cup finely diced carrots
- 1 cup shredded cabbage
- ¼ cup finely diced tomato
- 2 cups diced mushrooms
- ½ cup Brussels sprouts
- 2/3 clove garlic, minced
- 1 cup unsalted vegetable stock
- Salt and pepper
- 3.5 oz. extra firm tofu
- ¼ teaspoon caraway seeds
- ¾ tablespoons cider vinegar

Directions

- In a large saucepan, combine all the ingredients. Bring to a boil then simmer for thirty five to forty minutes. Stir occasionally until tender.

Halibut Teriyaki

Ingredients

- 3.5 oz. halibut fillet
- ½ tablespoon olive oil, divided
- ¾ cup chopped bok choy
- 1/8 cup teriyaki sauce
- ½ teaspoon minced garlic
- 1 finely chopped leeks
- 2 teaspoons lemon herb seasoning
- 2 cups baby spinach
- ¼ cup mandarin orange sections – in water (drained)
- ½ tablespoon vinegar
- 1 cup cauliflower

Directions

- Put ½-teaspoon olive oil in baking dish. Add teriyaki sauce and halibut. Cover and bake at 325°F for thirty minutes. Heat 1 teaspoon of olive oil in a skillet.

- Add leeks, seasoning, bok choy, and garlic. Cook over high heat until tender.

- Steam the cauliflower. Serve the halibut on top of bok choy, together with mandarin oranges and spinach. Drizzle with vinegar.

Tuna Broccoli

Ingredients

- 3 oz. light tuna chunks in water, drained

- 2 cups small broccoli, chopped

- 1 tablespoon chopped walnuts

- 1 teaspoon extra virgin olive oil

- Extra spicy seasoning

Directions

- Mix tuna, broccoli, and seasoning then warm in the microwave. Afterwards, sprinkle on the walnuts and drizzle with olive oil.

Chicken Tomatoes

Ingredients

- 3 oz. deboned and skinned chicken breast
- 1 teaspoon olive oil
- 2 cups chopped mushrooms
- 1 can diced tomatoes (14.5oz.)
- ¼ teaspoon red pepper flakes
- 8 oz. canned sauerkraut

Directions

- Sauté chicken in a pan and add pepper flakes, mushrooms, tomatoes, and sauerkraut.
- Simmer for ten minutes, or until chicken and mushroom are cooked.
- Drizzle with oil.

Beef and Broccoli Stir Fry

Ingredients

- 1 tablespoon olive oil

- 1 chopped onion

- Half cloves crushed garlic

- 100 grams lean beef

- 1 cup broccoli flowerets

- Salt and pepper

Directions

- Sauté garlic and onion in oil then add the beef. Stir-fry until cooked then add the broccoli. Add salt and pepper. Simmer for a few minutes until cooked.

Salmon with Tofu

Ingredients

- 1 slice of salmon
- 1 clove chopped garlic
- 1 medium onion
- Salt and pepper
- ½ cup tofu
- ½ cup spring onion
- 1 tablespoon olive oil

Directions

- Sauté onion and garlic in oil then add salmon and tofu. Add salt and pepper. Add spring onion when salmon and tofu are both cooked.

Indian Tuna Salad

Ingredients

- 2 tablespoons light mayonnaise
- 3 ½ oz. light tuna chunks in water
- 1 tablespoon freshly squeezed lemon juice
- 2 teaspoons curry powder
- 1 stalk celery, sliced thinly
- ¼ teaspoon of salt
- 2 tablespoons minced red onion
- 1 chopped red apple
- 2 cup torn lettuce
- 2 tablespoons red grapes

Directions

- Whisk the curry powder, salt, mayonnaise, and lemon juice in a medium-sized bowl.
- Drain the tuna then stir in the mayo mix.
- Add red onion, celery, red apple, and grapes.
- Place a bed of lettuce over a plate then top with the tuna salad.

Garlic Pork

Ingredients

- 1 pork chop
- Olive oil
- ¼ cup crushed garlic
- 2 tablespoon soy sauce

Directions

- Heat oil in a pan then add the garlic. Add the pork when the garlic turns brown. Season it with soy sauce.

Chapter 5 DELIGHTFUL DESSERTS

Banana Pudding

Ingredients

- 2 oz. tofu

- 2 almonds

- 1/3 banana

Preparation

- Mix all the ingredients in a blender until smooth.

Yogurt Delight

Ingredients

- 1 cup plain yogurt
- ½ teaspoon protein powder
- 1 teaspoon fructose
- Dash of almond, vanilla, and orange
- 2/3 teaspoon olive oil

Directions

- Stir in all ingredients until smooth

Hotcake

Ingredients

- 1/8 cup cottage cheese
- 1 egg
- 1/8 teaspoon salt
- 1/8 cup flour

Directions

- Beat yolks until thick then add the cottage cheese.
- Stir salt and flour into the beaten egg.
- Cook on medium heat.

Chocolate Pudding

Ingredients

- 1 to 2 squares chocolate

- 1 package of silken tofu

Directions

- Melt the chocolate squares in the microwave then let them cool.

- Whip a portion of the tofu in a blender until smooth then add the warm chocolate.

- Add the remaining tofu and keep blending until smooth.

Chocolate Parfait

Ingredients

- ¼ teaspoon vanilla

- 1/8 teaspoon cocoa powder

- 1/4 cup non-fat yogurt

- 1/8 teaspoon agave nectar

- ¼ cup blueberries

- ¼ cup raspberries

- ¾ tablespoons walnuts

Directions

- Mix the first four ingredients in a bowl until they are well combined.

- Add two tablespoons of yogurt into a tall glass. Top with some of the berries until all yogurt and berries are used. Sprinkle with walnuts then refrigerate before serving.

Fruity Summer Shake

Ingredients

- ¾ cup fat free yogurt

- 1/3 cup frozen strawberries

- 1/3 avocado

- 2/3 cup frozen cranberries

- 1/3 cup frozen peaches

- 1/8 cup 2% milk

Directions

- Except for milk, put everything in the blender. Blend slowly while adding milk. Continue until smooth.

Conclusion

I hope you enjoyed all the recipes you've discovered from this cooking resource.

Lastly, kindly share this book with your friends and have fun preparing new, exciting Zone-diet dishes together.

Thank you and good luck!

A.J. Parker Books:

1.

Why Should I Eat Organic Foods? The Pro's, The Con's, & Everything You'd Want To Know

2.

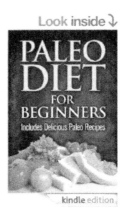

Paleo Diet For Beginners

3.

Macrobiotic Diet: Eat Healthy, Get Healthy, Improve Your Health - Includes Delicious Recipes

4.

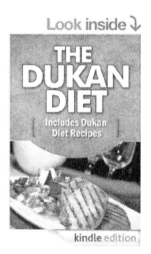

The Dukan Diet: Includes Dukan Diet Recipes To Get Started Immediately

5.

Zone Diet: Includes Zone Diet Recipes

6.

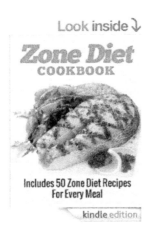

Zone Diet Cookbook - Includes 50 Zone Diet Recipes For Every Meal

Printed in Great Britain
by Amazon

18983750R00037